How Communism and Socialism Work

By

Robert Villegas

How Communism and Socialism Work

By Robert Villegas

Printed in the United States of America.

ISBN: 9798445677963

Imprint: Independently published

Robertv1989@outlook.com

Photo Credit: Photo by Pixabay: https://www.pexels.com/photo/adventure-backlit-dawn-dusk-207896/

Robert Villegas Social Media Addresses

Blog: Bobby's Book Shelf https://bobbysbookshelf.blogspot.com/
Audible: Robert Villegas Audible Books https://www.audible.com/search?keywords=Robert+Villegas&k=
Top Selling Books: Top Selling Books: Robert Villegas

https://robertvillegas2.blogspot.com/2024/10/top-selling-books-by-robert-villegas.html
Goodreads: Robert Villegas Goodreads
https://www.goodreads.com/search?q=Robert+Villegas&qid=hpiuucIJ3O
Amazon: Robert Villegas on Amazon
https://amzn.to/48flNvl
Instagram: rville9755
META/Facebook: Robert Villegas on Facebook
https://www.facebook.com/profile.php?id=61570138561465
Minds @Robertv1989
Gab @V4Vendata
GETTR @V4Vendata
WIMKIN Robert Villegas
X: @RobertVillegasJ
Parler: @V4Vendata
Threads: rville9755

Table of Contents

Dedicated to
Bill Childs

How Communism and Socialism Work

Introduction

In 1990, I had the opportunity to vacation for a week in Berlin, Germany. It was during this time that the Berlin Wall was coming down and citizens of both East and West Germany, as well as tourists like me, came to the wall to participate in the ritual of "hammers and chisels" that enabled us to be part of bringing the wall down.

For me, this was a critical moment as I walked along the wall. I met a gentleman who rented me a hammer and chisel so I could bang out pieces of the wall to take home as souvenirs of my trip.

It made little difference to me that the sky on that day was overcast. What was important to me was the humanity that was celebrating freedom for the first time in their lives. These people had always rejected communism in their lives, but they could not speak about it. They harbored a deep-seated anger at what coercion from the Soviet Union and East Germany's Stasi had done to their lives. How could anyone again promote communist lies and try to destroy capitalism?

As I stood there, getting ready to chip off my pieces of the wall, I engaged in conversation with some of the Germans around me. One gentleman, in particular, explained that he was a West German citizen and did not remember a time when the wall was not a subject of conversation. He had experienced the freedom and prosperity of the west and understood the significance of the new times in which he lived. He was fully aware that Soviet-style communism and the Stasi government of East Germany had failed the people trapped behind the wall. He knew the failures of communism.

As I walked around the streets of East Berlin, I noticed that the conditions of the East were inferior to those of the West. I noticed it in the people (East Germans' faces were streaked with worry lines that exposed the failure of their social infrastructure). They were poorly groomed, unwashed, and wearing old, torn clothing, while West Germans were well-groomed, well-washed, and their clothes were freshly laundered and new.

These differences between East and West exposed the failures of the communist state and the success of the freer capitalist state of the west. The main difference, however, was the self-confidence of the Westerners who were not psychologically oppressed by the spying of the state like East Berliners were. Poverty was the economic condition of the east and despair was its emotion.

Later, sitting at a bar near my home in Bad Soden, I talked to a prosperous German about the people of the east. He informed me of a family he knew that was allowed to invite its cousins to visit them in the west. These visitors were disheveled and uncut east Germans

astonished at the quality and newness of the homes and furnishings of their western cousins.

They saw these furnishings and appliances as examples of the corruption of the west. They assumed that communist propaganda was true; that western prosperity had been stolen from the east by greedy capitalists. One day, the prosperous Western cousins came home to find their houses empty of furnishings and appliances – with a note left for them, "You have stolen from us for decades. It is our turn now."

Things have changed in the world since then. Everywhere in America, school children are taught to hate capitalism while its abundance is destroyed by leftist policies. As in the past, the west swallowed the lie that socialism and communism are *the* moral systems while capitalism is corrupt and exploitative of the individual.

The advocates of socialism and communism assert, on principle, that the individual belongs to the state and the state can do whatever it wants to him. Contrast these coercive governments with capitalist systems based upon the individual, and you will understand why communism and socialism oppose capitalism. The proponents of these coercive systems do not want the people to know that force and capitalism are opposites, and especially, that capitalism is superior to communism and socialism by at least a factor of 100 to 1.

In fact, it is the coercive nature of communism and socialism that makes these systems unworkable; and it is the lack of coercion in capitalism that creates the abundance and prosperity normally associated with it. It is also the freedoms of capitalism that move dictators and technocrats to want to do away with it. As long as capitalism flourishes, as Marcuse averred, there is no way that communism and socialism can advance beyond it. This is because they are inferior systems relative to the individual.

The fundamental difference between communism/socialism and capitalism is founded on differing views on how society should (or should not) manage the means of production. Today's progressives (socialists, communists, and fascists) think that society has the responsibility to manage and direct the process of production by owning or dictating the use of property, machines, factories, and capital. The premise is that man and society are owned by the government and that society should manage them for the sake of the tribe or collective.

The capitalist view is that the means of production, and all property, should be owned by individuals and that they are the tools that the individual uses to benefit his life; that man has the right and freedom to direct production without interference from authority figures and/or government.

ASMR[1]: "I'll tell you a secret. Most people don't really know what capitalism is. Most people don't really know what socialism is. But most people are not capitalists because they don't have

---

[1] Autonomous Sensory Meridian Response (or AOC (and Biden) whispering)

capitalist money. Unionize your workplace. Start a worker cooperative. If it is too extreme for working people to own the means of production, why is it ok for private billionaires to own the means of production?"

Answer: There is no secret about any of this drivel. It is based on Marxist nonsense that is known around the world. Unionization and "workers' cooperatives" are aspects of both communism and socialism. What she is saying is that most people don't know that these "worker" concepts are aspects of communism and socialism. She implies that they are good, but many people don't recognize them as communist or socialist. She is declaring that others (but not her) don't know that they admire socialism and communism because they admire many aspects of the two systems.

What is the fallacy here? In truth, if most people do not know what capitalism is, it is because of the negative propaganda about capitalism regularly spewed by socialist teachers throughout our entire educational system and even in the media. Teachers and journalists constantly disparage capitalism's positive features in order to declare that capitalism is exploitative and evil (which it is not); and they have no problem misleading school children and the public. This is because communists and socialists in our schools are hateful, spiteful and ignorant about the benefits of capitalism and they know (subconsciously) that they can never defeat capitalism unless they lie about it.

AOC's basic mistake is her confusion over morality and economics. She declares that both capitalism and billionaires are evil without offering a moral justification except the lie that they are intent on hurting people and stealing from them. Despite the fact that it isn't true, it is such an easy lie to tell because altruism guilts people into accepting it. She merely trots out the old bromides of "rich versus poor" class differences while she pretends to be presenting economic (Marxist) proofs that have no basis in science or economics.

The attacks on capitalism by leftist environmentalists are intended to destroy capitalism – this requires the destruction of industrial society despite the fact that they claim they are merely looking for "better" machines to replace fossil fuel-based machines. Capitalism operates on the basis of supply and demand which leads to the best, most efficient machines. To replace fossil fuel-based machines will lead, almost immediately, to less production, higher prices, economic restrictions and eventually, to mass hunger and death. You cannot get rid of an efficient industrial process by fiat and expect that better products will come along. The green new deal is a recipe for murder.

As a spokesperson for socialism and communism, AOC does not realize that if you are living in a capitalist economy, your pay comes from productive corporations and billionaire investors; you can even borrow money and invest it to start your own business; you can and do participate in the production of the capitalist industrial society (that operates on the principle of supply and demand). You are a capitalist because you benefit from the capitalist system. In fact, you earn capitalist money every time you cash your paycheck.

The key mistakes that AOC makes is to think that there is something evil about the capitalist system and something good about communism and socialism. Yet, she gives no argument to support her assumptions about the morality of these systems. She merely hurls ridicule upon capitalism and pretends that communism and socialism never killed people in the millions. Yet, she declares it is moral for workers to create their own "cooperatives" without capital (or by taking capital from the billionaires) and that it is improper (and should be illegal) for billionaires to start businesses with their own capital.

Marx had set up the capitalist era as a battle between wage earner and profit maker. He asserted that the economic class struggle between these two classes, would usher in a synthesis that would result in socialism. Marx's major fallacy on this issue is that he sets up a false and unrealistic dichotomy that he couches under the metaphysic of historical materialism which is a rationalistic fallacy.

In truth, under capitalism, every man is a businessperson, contrary to AOC. Every man, including the wage earner, competes for profit as a de facto entrepreneur. There are no classes in a capitalistic system. In fact, capitalism is the solution to class systems, the answer to the mercantilist system of class dominance of commerce. AOC and her communist friends are treating capitalism as if it were mercantilism and imperialism. In capitalism, every man is rich depending on the amount of work and efficiency he is capable of realizing. Capitalism is individualism while communism and socialism create a class struggle between the elite (murderous) rulers and the workers. Communism and socialism both exploit the workers and the intelligent people in society. They foster and impose poverty upon the workers by demanding that the productive people sacrifice their work and money to the state. This leaves a class of administrators who live off the work of the people and a class of workers who must live in poor housing, shop at stores with empty shelves, and experience hunger.

The labor movement under communism and socialism would never have mushroomed into any sort of revolution, had it not been for social agitators, false interpretations of Marxist intellectuals and government protection of labor. It is a tribute to capitalism that despite AOC's desire to resurrect the labor movement, there is little interest today in taking over factories. Marx's theory of class struggle has fallen apart, and along with it, the idea that communism is the next historical phase after capitalism.

Despite the fact that we are not now living under capitalism, A O C implies that any economic system which has a mere semblance of private property must be based upon the fraudulent use of capital. This is decidedly untrue. In fact, whenever you corrupt a truly capitalist system, through violations of individual rights, you have made the system into a coercive society. To deny or restrict freedom is to deny or restrict free trade and the benevolence of capitalist society.

Ours is AOC's society now because she and her associates have made it into a socialist/fascist society through the intrusion of anti-capitalist elements. AOC is criticizing as evil the very society that she and her fellow socialists have made. To that extent, her socialism *is* evil and deserves to be restored to its original capitalist condition. In fact, all of the problems that socialists associate with capitalism are actually features of socialism, the very society that AOC and her associates have made.

It is true that many people do not understand what socialism is. This is because of the indoctrination they received from socialist teachers. Such teachers, eager to advance the coercive nature of socialism and communism (without telling the students about it), lie to students about the promise of human sacrifice. Likewise, unions and worker cooperatives do not save society or make it pure in any sense. Such institutions are anti-capitalist, and they destroy production by robbing the workers of their wages and making sacrificial victims of them.

The idea of the workers owning the factories is based upon an anti-capitalist prejudice that has failed repeatedly. It wrongly assumes that the machines and factories are forces of nature that can be magically organized by the workers. Under such a false utopian scheme, the workers will always come up short. The only things that cause the victory of socialism are the false notions that capitalism is unfair. Capitalism fails because socialist programs fail. Socialists blame capitalism for the failures of socialism, and this causes people to think that socialism is the solution. In fact, socialism fails repeatedly. We need to get our educational system straight in order to save our children and our society from the scourges of socialism, communism, historical materialism, and pseudo-science. Individualism and capitalism are the solutions for communism and socialism.

Critical Theory

Critical theorists (communists and socialists) around the world ignore the fact that socialism and communism are coercive systems. Their lies are sold to people as if they were magical and moral. In coercive societies like theirs, they think, it is proper for the state to make men sacrifice. For them, the state is superior to "mere" men. These judgments of critical theorists are, at base, pseudo-scientific prejudices that misrepresent reality. Indeed, when they cry that they will destroy class-based societies, they don't realize that coercive societies are the creators of class societies.

"Starting in the 1930s, the Frankfurt School was in dialogue with both capitalism and Marxism. Rejecting Marxist determinism and Russia's bureaucratic and totalitarian regime, this school of thought comprising Max Horkheimer, Theodor Adorno, Erich Fromm, Herbert Marcuse and others reduced the role of economics by integrating it with political questions. In addition, criticism was broadened to include psychologized, Freudian, versions of alienation, working class fragmentation, and even family issues."[2]

Communism is the system fostered by Karl Marx, Friedrich Engels and millions of "revolutionaries" who claimed they had the answer for the world's problems. In modern times, such people are the critical theorists (and critical race theorists) who base their views upon Marxist metaphysical and political premises. For them, it is moral for society to fight against capitalist productive people (who are the true moral people) and force them to give up their values. There is nothing moral about Marxist calls for property expropriation.

Marx and Engels proposed that the class struggle was a universal cosmic (metaphysical) principle that harkened the coming of a movement away from capitalism and toward a "worker's democracy" that was nothing more than outright human sacrifice. Marx and Engels took advantage of the globally accepted notion that men should live for each other and submit to the power of

---

[2] Critical Theory: Frankfurt School, Characteristics of Critical Theory and Critical Theorists Article shared by Puja Mandal Source: https://www.yourarticlelibrary.com/essay/sociology-essay/critical-theory-frankfurt-school-characteristics-of-critical-theory-and-critical-theorists/39913

the state. This grossly improper view led to the opinion that men should sacrifice for the state rather than live for themselves.

Marx and Engels have had a virtual monopoly on the meaning of the Industrial Revolution. Their theory was that the Industrial Revolution was the antithesis of feudalism and that it emerged as a result of historical materialism which was a reinterpretation of Hegel's "thesis, antithesis, and synthesis" metaphysic. For Marxists, every period of history was the product of the class struggle and capitalism had within it the seeds of a new system—socialism. They then proceeded to create narratives about class inequalities and other imperfections in capitalism, showing that the working classes would usher in the new socialist system, that capitalism was dying, and socialism was the wave of the future.

Marx and Engels were decidedly wrong. Hegel was wrong about history and the theory of an historical process was pure mysticism. Finally, their criticisms of capitalism were gross distortions based upon wishful thinking and a disregard for facts.

But Marx and Engels had one thing going for them (if not truth): They were operating within the mainstream of philosophical debate. Their theories merely picked up on the work done by Feuerbach *and* Hegel, to mention a few. Their romantic promise of a sunlit future for mankind under socialism was a false promise. This established them as revolutionaries for a "good" cause because it was attached to what has been universally regarded as noble (altruism). It became chic to be a socialist. Historical inaccuracy and philosophical incompetence did not deter those who mistakenly saw in socialism's advocacy, a chance to be in on the future.

It is within this atmosphere of intellectual irresponsibility that socialism has grown into what it always was: an effort to destroy, loot and murder; legally permitted to those who knew only the power of destruction. Around the world, socialism is baring its teeth, destroying anything that resembles capitalism, proclaiming hatred for anything that is the product of human intelligence.

But, even after centuries of Marxist lies, we hear little about socialism's failures. We hear only that socialism is the wave of the future. The critical theorists are still at it. Critical Theorist Marcuse declared: "The growing opposition to the global dominion of corporate capitalism is confronted by the sustained power of this dominion: its economic and military hold in the four continents, its neocolonial empire, and most important, its unshaken capacity to subject the majority of the underlying population to its overwhelming productivity and force..."[3]

One must wonder: if capitalism is so powerful that socialism is always on the defense, then how can socialism be superior? How can a system that will disappear have a military hold or the ability to subject the majority to anything, or even to bring productivity *and* force? The answer can only be that socialism repeatedly fails against capitalism because it is inferior to capitalism.

It is socialism that is militaristic, that enslaves people and destroys production through force. It is capitalism that has the ability to defend

---

[3] An Essay on Liberation by Herbert Marcuse

itself against socialism and communism. It is capitalism that makes people free. It is capitalism that is productive and efficient for the worker. It is capitalism that creates the worker and makes him happy. Indeed, today, there is less excuse for the advocacy of socialism than for capitalism. The historical process is being "nudged" by a socialist gun.

In fact, throughout the early Industrial Revolution, it was coercive governments that ruined commerce for millions of people. Government restrictions and wars contributed to poor currency systems and unemployment. Many of the "evils" attributed to the Industrial Revolution were actually remnants of the primitive stages of production that were at that time disappearing. Even the existence of inhumane working conditions for children cannot be attributed to capitalism, but to the gross negligence of the owners who did not understand the new capitalist systems under which they were working. Children were employed in many of these industries, not as a way of buying cheaper labor, but because most people over the age of puberty could not adjust to the mechanical requirements of the new industries (again, the blame should be on the remnants of the primitive feudal systems).

Finally, we must distinguish between what is taken to be capitalism today and older classical theories of economics that were disappearing while society transitioned to capitalism. Today, major corporations are not capitalist entities but products of the pragmatist philosophy that declares "perception is reality". This is not capitalism but fascism. It is technocracy and central planning. Today's major corporations have succumbed to the call for globalism, Confucius Institutes and doing business in China.

Classical theories of capitalism, on the other hand, are a product of the ideas of Adam Smith, Henry Hazlitt, Ludwig von Mises, Ayn Rand and others who understood the values of laissez faire capitalism that declared the principle of "hands off" to be the proper policy of capitalist governments.

Marxism's Basic Flaw

"Engels explains in his brilliant essay *Labour in the Transition of Ape to Man* how the upright stance freed the hands, which had originally evolved as an adaptation for climbing trees, for other purposes. The production of stone tools represented a qualitative leap, giving our ancestors an evolutionary advantage. But even more important was the strong sense of community, collective production, and social life, which in turn was closely connected to the development of language."[4]

This premise, of course, is wrong. What separates man from other mammals is that he *thinks*, and it is this characteristic that helped him evolve into modern man. Man's first tool (that caused his advance) is his mind. Man uses his mind to perceive, to cogitate, conceptualize, to develop knowledge, to keep and use that knowledge to improve his life.

Marx and Engels lived during a period when anthropology was a young and developing science. From all over the world, the evidence

____

[4] The Ideas of Karl Marx by Alan Woods Source: https://www.marxist.com/karl-marx-130-years.htm

from new digs produced tools, and an entirely new set of conclusions that declared that man's nature is to think in order to survive, and that his thinking involves alternatives and choices.

The real issue is the hierarchy of knowledge with his mind answering the question, "What comes first?" Man's mind asked the first questions: "What is real and how do I know it?" The answer is "The real is what I observe and I know it by observing reality, defining concepts and learning the rules of thinking, logic (induction and deduction)." From this comes the sciences which leads to the tools that yield survival.

By making man into a subconscious tool maker (who had no mind), Marx and Engels resorted to a rationalistic conclusion that the class struggle was the essential conflict of history, that every historical period could be understood only by focusing on class struggles. From Feuerbach, Marx got the idea of interpreting what people say and do, in economic terms, and fitting them into what sides of the struggle to which they belonged. Freud also took the same lead from Feuerbach and used this method to analyze people's actions and words in the psychological sense. Thus, Marx had a powerful tool of intimidation against those who disagreed with him. He merely called them Bourgeoisie. That was enough to silence and convert many who did not want to be on the "losing" side.

But this idea about the class struggle could only be valid if Marx's claim that socialism will inevitably win over capitalism is correct. Of interest also, is Marx's view of religion as an "opiate." He felt that frustrations over human wants and needs were so strong that people inevitably projected another better world where all wants were satisfied. For Marx, religion failed in providing that world despite the fact that socialism too failed at bringing heaven (utopia).

This utopian argument has little to reveal about human nature since most religions formed centuries ago and are not reformed daily (like progressive policies); and since, today, even in advanced countries, religion exists. Indeed, even in irreligious societies a semblance of religion is still alive through the rationalism found in modern philosophy.

The real issue is not that man creates religion (which he does); but those who fall for Marx's arguments about religion are as guilty as he is of altering history to vent their own frustrations on believers. Marx was merely trying to discredit religion in favor of his own more or less religious views. The fact is that we know little about how religion originated. We do know that religion is self-perpetuating while also being culturally inherited. This means it creates, over time, psychologies that accept it without thought.

What is communism and how can it replace religion? How does communism create poverty, hunger, alcoholism, and genocide? The answer is that communism is a form of altruism that has always been the essential moral philosophy of most major religions. Altruism, whether in the form of religion or in the form of a secular view, is a moral philosophy that declares self-interest to be a crime. Both forms of altruism (communism and religion) claim that the essence of moral living is to dedicate your life to others and their well-being. Altruism makes the individual into a slave by making self-interest into a sin. This makes communism a lie that destroys not only the mind of man (through indoctrination) but also the very existence of truth and reality. The Marxist maxim, "from each according to his ability, to each according to his need" is the essential expression of altruism, the moral basis of Marxist religious premises.

When a society makes sacrifice into its leading principle, its critical theorist supporters declare that something magical happens; society transitions to communism; people work for the sake of society and everything becomes flowers and roses; people are happy, and all their needs are met. This is why altruism is fostered by communism and becomes the false solution for capitalism.

In fact, what society "gives" to some people, it must "take" from other people and this *taking* exploits worthy, productive people for the sake of the unworthy and unproductive people. This fact is why socialism and communism always fail – over time, eventually, productive people in society refuse to participate in their own enslavement and this causes the downward economic decline that is common in coercive states such as fascism, communism, and socialism.

This eventual refusal of productive people to support their nonproductive fellow citizens is not done out of hatred or a desire to harm the poor. It is not done because capitalists want to exploit the poor. It is the natural result of altruism's imposition upon them; it is the result of being treated unfairly. Altruism is not a sweet-smelling flower; it is a trap that enslaves the individual and consigns him to perennial servitude.

Communism and Human Sacrifice

The philosophy that created communism, human sacrifice, came from modern philosophy as it developed from the ideas of thinkers such as Hegel, Hume, and Kant. But both Marxism and Christianity are based upon human sacrifice, and this is a critical issue that few people have noticed.

Christianity has always preached sacrifice with one of its key premises that Jesus sacrificed his life for mankind. Jesus was the ultimate sacrifice who gave his life to exonerate man for his sins. As I have written elsewhere, the sacrifice of Jesus was an example for how men should live their lives, sacrificing for society. It was the writers of the gospel who took human sacrifice to the ultimate level by doubling down on sacrifice, recommending that when men sacrifice to one degree, they should go farther and sacrifice to the ultimate degree.[5]

Modern philosophy took human sacrifice, in the form of altruism, to an even more demanding level in the form of the categorical imperative to duty. The culprit, ultimately, was Kant.

---

[5] The Parable of the Good Samaritan

Ian Heckman declares:

"Kant was, in many respects, an anti-metaphysician, meaning that he rejected traditional metaphysics, including issues related to nominalism. He thought that we could neither know of nor conceive of something like the existence of abstract universals which exist outside of time and space. These sorts of things are out of the bounds of our experience. He thought any attempt to prove the existence or non-existence of these things would end up in error and contradiction. He also believed that we couldn't prove the existence of God for similar reasons, though he thought we should believe in God for moral ones."[6]

To counter the nominalism of modern philosophy, writer George Orwell teaches us about the Big Lie, the constant repetition of an untruth that turns the lie into a Deweyan false promise that "perception is reality." Marx, following suit, declares that the meanings of words can be transformed into their opposites (which declaration destroys the mind and turns it

---

[6] https://www.quora.com/Was-Kant-a-nominalist?share=1

into a false quest for a false promise that utopia can be reality).

The solution to the persistent "emergencies" created by Marxists, is for the individual to sacrifice for the collective. Under this scheme, we have "reverse think" through which peace is war, love is hate, force is voluntary, information is misinformation, and sacrifice is the good. The distance between the sacrifice of Jesus to save man and the sacrifice of man to save society is advanced by modern society to new heights of self-destruction.

The demand for human sacrifice today (also called equity) is the deception that keeps people constantly reacting to fabricated conspiracies that switch whenever leaders need to send people over the precipice. Old defunct causes become new causes through the clever use of different words, concepts, and principles. With the new communism, everything changes, and the lowly citizen learns that man cannot know, cannot get along, and cannot project the future. All is confusion in a world of deliberately switching truths and principles. One thing that never changes is the demand that man should sacrifice his values for others. This holds for religion, communism, socialism, and fascism. Human sacrifice is the perennial demand.

Marxists know that communism and socialism are inferior to capitalism. They know that in order to advance coercive society, they must lie that capitalism is exploitation of the worker; that it "forces" man to give up his values for the sake of the rich capitalist.

Marxism maliciously divides men into warring groups that can never reconcile without violent revolution. Today, they are against white. Tomorrow they will be against black. Today, they defend "native groups" and tomorrow they forget about them. The only constant for Marxists is that they should always trust the power of government regardless of what it does to impoverish society. What Marxism does, essentially, is criticize the individual (capitalism) on behalf of whatever collectives it thinks it can "defend". It has no problem fabricating collectives in order to provoke anti-capitalism.

Starting with Marx's class warfare (collectives), Marxism fabricates as many collectives as possible (ethnicism, ethno-centrism, racism, tribalism, workers enclaves, etc.) in order to give its agitating revolutionaries the arguments they need to bring capitalism (individualism) down.

The problem with communists and socialists is that, because of their altruistic premises, they pretend that they are the "good guys". Why do they want to destroy the most affluent and positive social system ever created by man? It is not because they want a better society – they do not. It is not because they think communism and socialism create abundance – they do not. Simply put, they must destroy capitalism because it creates abundance. They can't win the future for central planning and technocracy while there is a system in place that is superior to their own failed and failing policies. They must cover up their own failures in order to cover up the fact that they can neither lead nor govern. Neither communism nor socialism provide the means for competent and successful leadership of society. They only teach envious men how to destroy society so they can rule with an iron fist, engage in social agitation, and genocidal murder.

Capitalism is not the pariah system the Marxists declare it to be. This lie about capitalism is a reversal of objective truth. It turns people into martinets who become rigid fighters, community organizers, and street activists intent on destroying capitalism. Marxist leaders distort history and understanding in order to create a blind movement against prosperity and affluence. If people were to discover that capitalism is *the* answer to the coercive state, then the communist dream of enslaving people would have been lost.

Let us examine how communism works:

First, communists must build up the idea of human sacrifice and make it into "our deepest value"[7]. They give glowing praise to the idea of living for others. They tell us that everything in the promised future will be love and kindness, and no one will want for anything. This is how they use words about "love of humanity" to enslave people.

But it does not add up. The idea that sacrifice yields positive results is a lie. It is not, as the dupes think, a good idea poorly implemented.

---

[7] For instance, when Obama and his minions talked about American values, they were talking about the "value" of human sacrifice. This is not what the Founding Fathers meant.

Sacrifice for the collective is a bad idea that yields bad results. In fact, the results of communism/socialism are so bad that millions have died for them and been killed by them.

How did this happen? Any individual who thinks that government has no right to steal his or her values, is automatically branded as a selfish monster who must be punished for thinking of himself first. He or she is sent to reeducation camps, prison camps and/or murdered along with millions of fellow citizens.

The idea of human sacrifice (as a moral premise) came from prehistoric times and religious premises. Marxists had to eliminate religion in order to steal from it the social application of human sacrifice. In fact, they were the proponents of human sacrifice in the same way that Christians hanged their god on a cross as a sacrifice for the world.

The Marxists stole the idea of human sacrifice from the Christians because they understood the gimmick. They understood that they, like the Christians, could manipulate men into giving up their values, and at the same time replace the Christian "spiritual" heaven (that awaited death) with a utopia that would happen during life. Sacrifice to the state was merely another form of sacrifice for mankind like the sacrifice of Jesus on the cross.

The Marxists used sacrifice as a weapon of manipulation because they knew the Christians had been effective in using it during their time. They called religion an opiate, not because they (the Marxists) were "scientific" by any means. That was a ruse – religion, in the form of human sacrifice, was the opiate the communists and socialists wanted to use for their own sakes. This is why they declared themselves logical and scientific – but it was pseudo-science, not true science, that made them want to burn churches and Bibles, kill religious belief, use hate speech, disseminate misinformation, and put people in concentration camps. Then, to top it off, they had to accuse capitalism of doing all the things that they, the socialists and communists, were doing. They had to get rid of religion in order to make communism and socialism into the "true faith".

We must come to grips with the fact that altruism has never been a viable solution for society. There has never been a proof that altruism produces good for society or that it is good for men and especially good for the poor. When you destroy the productive (good people), you destroy society (and even the poor). The only justification for altruism is "God demands it," or "society is more important than the people who produce things." Both of these notions are untrue.

Pragmatism

As the failures of socialism and communism manifest themselves, we move from the destruction of dissent to the destruction of society. Pragmatism and blind activism come to the fore and running society becomes a "magic act" designed to fool and manipulate people into believing in the myth of coercion. Nominalism, magic words, blind feelings and (once again) the Big Lie give people a philosophy that does not work. Leaders double down on the falsehoods and continue to indoctrinate students by destroying knowledge. Kant, Dewey, and Comte give us indeterminacy, pragmatism and logical positivism in order to keep young people in the fold and hide the truth that coercion is not a positive factor in society.

Technocrats assume they have the knowledge needed to create positive results for society. They consider themselves to be the pragmatic doers and button pushers who know how to change minds by changing reality under the premise that perception is reality.[8]

---

[8] Perception is not reality.

The truth is that technocrats do not know how to plan society. They lack the knowledge and abilities to decide what people should think and should do. It is impossible for a technocrat to control the thoughts and opinions of millions of people; and it is impossible to be smarter than the countless millions who each know more about their own lives than any technocrat could ever know. Communism and socialism fail because the technocrats of central planning coercively deny to people the freedom they need to make their own decisions. More importantly, people know, instinctively, when pretentious blowhards are manipulating them.

As time goes by, coming generations of socialists and communists will stick to the lie of altruism and sacrifice; they will insist that people must sacrifice and be punished for self-interest. What is unmentioned is that there is no end to the call for sacrificing. There is never a thought of ever stopping it; even when sacrifice leads to mass murder and economic depression over millions of people. In fact, when one demand for sacrifice spends itself in failure, the call for more sacrifice gets ever louder. There is never a thought about the possibility that human sacrifice should end –

that is just unthinkable. Rather than reason about the failures of coercion, admit that their quest for power is a false quest, and change their policies, they bring out the old saw of altruism and demand more of the failed policies. No one, hardly ever, concludes that human sacrifice is evil and destructive.

Politicians and technocrats will do everything they can to hide their own ineptitude by claiming that past communists and socialists corrupted the noble dream by killing people and forcing them to obey. They blame the failures of past governments on white people, capitalists, honest scientists, doctors, nurses, energy providers, and others. Further, they will declare that today's communists and socialists are really about being nice and fostering "democracy."

Even here, in this call for democracy, they continue the Big Lie of socialism and communism. They use the term "democracy" as a euphemism for "the people's vote". They declare that the leaders of the past did not do democracy right. They promise that *they* will be more kindly and respectful toward the people. They instruct children and adults about the enemies of democracy, individualists who live for themselves instead of "the people". Yet, they ignore the truth that dictators of the past also did their dirty deeds in the name of democracy.

This has been the pattern of excuse-making that always takes place when coercion leads to social failure. This releases the next generation of technocrats to experiment through the next iteration of failed socialism and communism.

Ad infinitum.

Conclusion

During early Marxist movements, communism was the new religion and like all religions, it was held as a matter of faith that the new god, society, was to be worshipped at all costs. Over time, however, the people victimized by communism, the sacrificers, learned that the strongest and most intelligent among them worked harder than the weakest and unintelligent. The more able people who worked in society eventually learned that they were required to take care of people who did not want to take care of themselves. When reality became obvious; when they realized they were working harder and government was not protecting them, they lost motivation and reduced their effort. This always happens in socialist / communist / fascist societies which explains why they always fail.

Communism and socialism were societies falsely based upon unity. But unity is merely a form of exploitation of the intelligent and able. Those who unite around altruism find themselves separated by conflict and war. The founding moral philosophy of both systems is mysticism and human sacrifice. It led to death for man and the destruction of the good.

Have you ever thought that altruism and human sacrifice might be the very ideas that have created the social problems that have plagued mankind for several centuries? Are we being poisoned by the failed ideas of communism and socialism?

I believe that communism and socialism will always fail because man does not survive by being weak and dependent upon others. Man survives by the use of his mind. The idea of making hard working people toil for someone who refuses to work is always going to result in a failed society. This goes for modern liberalism and progressivism.

Since man needs reason to survive, the act of punishing a man for using his mind is the essence of immorality and evil. That is why socialism and communism never work, and that is why the flowery promises of a coming abundance through coercive society are actually "magic words" that will never work. The indoctrination machine of the coercive state makes people think that something great will happen if they would only sacrifice. This is their Big Lie. Educators should be fired for giving young people this lie about the glory of the sacrificial state.

If you want to create an affluent society, you should establish individual rights in society and prohibit government from forcing people to sacrifice for others. You allow men to work freely and keep the results of their work. Individual rights are the prerequisites for human cooperation and productive activity. We have seen this work in the United States of America.

Government force and human sacrifice will not create a society of abundance and freedom. Certainly, we have a long way to go if we want to restore the promise of the Declaration of Independence, but this declaration can only come when men reject the idea that human sacrifice brings a better society. If you want a proper society, you must restore liberty. The following words are the means toward a proper society of happy and prosperous people.[9]

---

[9] Books of interest: *The Industrial Revolution 1760 – 1830,* by T. S. Ashton published by Oxford University Press, London, Oxford, New York. *What Marx Really Said* by H. B. Acton, Schocken Books, New York.

"We hold these truths to be self-evident, that all men are created equal, that they are endowed by their Creator with certain unalienable Rights, that among these are Life, Liberty and the pursuit of Happiness." - Preamble to the Declaration of Independence

I am an American writer from Weslaco, TX. I consider myself an independent philosopher with a strong influence from Objectivism, the philosophy of Ayn Rand. I have been studying and applying Objectivism to my writing and professional career since an early age.

I spent over twenty-seven years as a UPS executive in Indiana and worked in locations all over Europe such as Germany, England, and Spain. The system I designed in England was also used in Singapore. I also designed a Spanish language system in Madrid, Spain. At UPS I worked in various positions including Sales Manager, Call Center Manager and Telecommunications Manager. I was involved in helping to transition UPS from paper-based processes to computerized networks and digital record keeping. I worked with early digital technologies and was one of the first telecommunications managers to use technology for communicating to drivers while they were on their routes. My system caught the attention of our national group and influenced the development of the computerized clipboard now used at UPS and other companies. Other developments I made also had impacts on national UPS programs including account management, Gantt charting, complaint processing, and the development of outbound teleservices and sales departments.

My Business Philosophy developed through fifty plus years of experience in several fields including transportation and technology (UPS), telecommunications (PACER and UPS), call center management (UPS), sales management (UPS and others), Internet (Nextera and other companies), network design and implementation (UPS), technical and marketing writing (PACER and Nextera) and motorsport marketing (SponsorProAZ, Insight Marketing Group and several teams and drivers).

I studied free market economics through the writings of Mises, Hayek, Rand, Hazlitt, Friedman, and others and attended lectures by prominent economists. I also read voraciously and attended lectures about philosophy and the history of philosophy, business philosophy, sales history and methodology and worked as a marketing and technical writer, website designer and telecommunications manager as well as call center manager. During those years, I created presentations for high level investor meetings in NYC, Miami, San Francisco, Minneapolis, and many other locations. I designed trade show displays and traveled extensively designing and installing computer network software and call center networks in Munich, Frankfort, Dusseldorf, London, Singapore, and Madrid. I have written over 260 business plans, mostly for start-ups in Canada and the USA. I learned not only how to work for top level CEOs and VPs but also how to help them be successful.

Over the years, I was fortunate to have met influential people, saw several of the royals in London, and worked for well-known athletes, racing drivers and entertainment professionals and celebrities.

After leaving UPS, I started my own marketing and entertainment company specializing in writing sponsorship proposals for race car drivers, athletes, and celebrities. Clients included Johnny Parsons, Jeff Ward, Larry Foyt, Ike Runnels, Jimmy Ward, Pat Golden, Steve Newey, and Alexander Rossi to name a few. I also created successful sales presentations and marketing documents for companies in New York City, San Francisco, Boston, Sacramento, Chicago, Miami, Minneapolis, Vancouver BC, Florida (NASCAR) and other locations.

Since 2015, I have written about 106 books (and other publications) in areas such as novels, theater, religion, poetry, philosophy, Internet, Knowledge Management, and business with a strong emphasis on philosophy and philosophical analysis. I have also written successful grant proposals for organizations, earning millions of dollars for fire departments and charitable organizations.

I was mostly educated in Indiana and earned a Degree through the University of the State of NY (Albany) via an external degree program (when I came out of the military). I also served in the US Military as a communications specialist serving a tour of duty in Korea (during the Vietnam era) near the DMZ.

HELLO

1933-1945

I WRITE
What's your Superpower?

These four books comprise a system that can be used by both patients and counselors who are battling Alcoholism and Addiction. Based upon Mr. Villegas's own system developed during his struggle against alcoholism, this system includes:

Alcoholism and Addiction – A Secular Ten-Step Program

This groundbreaking book offers a secular approach to alcoholism unlike that offered by Alcoholics Anonymous. We recommend that every individual going for alcohol and drug-abuse counseling be given a copy of this book which contains the workbook and the two versions of The World's first drunk. http://amzn.to/2md6R9w $3.45 Kindle $11.95 softcover

The Secular Ten-Step Program Workbook

This booklet covers the program developed by Mr. Villegas. It is designed as a workbook with blank spaces for the patient to write his own thoughts as he takes each of the ten steps. Order one copy for each patient in counseling. http://amzn.to/2IrHimS $4.49 Kindle $6.95 softcover

The World's First Drunk – With Counselor Talking Points

This booklet is designed for the counselor as he works with patients during individual or group therapy. It contains helpful tips on discussing the life story of the man who invented alcohol. Order one copy for each patient in counseling. http://amzn.to/2I446Wr $2.99 Kindle $5.95 softcover

The World's First Drunk – Patient Version

This version of the short story contains empty spaces where the patient can answer questions about the life story of the man who invented alcohol. Order one copy for each counselor. http://amzn.to/2IdxBGb $2.99 Kindle $5.95 softcover.

These four books by Robert Villegas comprise some of the business books that he has written. As an executive working for several companies, he was able to develop these methods that will help anyone seeking to excel in the business world. These books are:

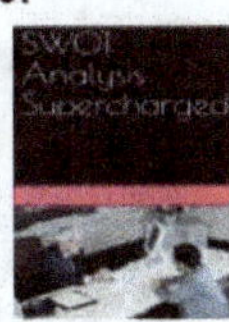

How to Be a Great Employee – and a Greater Manager

You cannot be a great manager without first being a great employee. And this is something that requires learning, experience and attitude. The attitude comes from you but the learning and experience you should acquire through diligent study and practice. http://amzn.to/2BqdG2i $3.99 Kindle $8.95 softcover

SWOT Analysis Supercharged

A SWOT Analysis is an objective look at the internal and external elements of your organization that impact your success or lack thereof. If done diligently, you will always have a handle on what you need to do to improve season after season. http://amzn.to/2BCAWYx $3.99 Kindle $6.95 softcover

The Five-Module Call Center Training System

The Five-Module Call Center Training System is designed to assist the Call Center Team Leader in helping his employees quickly upgrade their skills to an acceptable level. http://amzn.to/2B3Svj1 $3.99 Kindle $5.95 softcover

Website Development Methodology

Effective strategic marketing requires the ability to differentiate the website development organization and its deliverables from those of the competition. http://amzn.to/2DnYMqh $2.99 Kindle $12.95 softcover.

The Mark of Titus
Excerpts from the book Unkilling Jesus which highlight some of the key discoveries implied by new theories about the origin of the Jesus Myth. The idea that the Romans invented Christianity is the basic premise of new theories about the origin of Christianity .http://amzn.to/2itMCo0 $3.49 Kindle $5.95 softcover

Contra Religion
This book is designed as a "shorter" explanation of the ideas presented in my larger book, "Behind the Ritual Mask" which seeks to define fundamental principles of religion. I'm hoping this book will serve as a primer for the original book and spur an interest in reading it. http://amzn.to/2yWMSlx $3.99 Kindle $6.95 softcover

Is this the Face that Launched a Thousand Ships?
It was love at first sight. I saw her one day while watching a television program about King Tut, whose tomb had been discovered by Howard Carter years before. I was looking at the famous bust of a beautiful Egyptian Queen. https://amzn.to/3t487x3 $3.99 Kindle $7.95 softcover

The History of Altruism
The History of Altruism is a historical treatment of the development of altruism throughout time from the Paleolithic period to today. It tracks the development of self-sacrifice of primitive man to the advent of altruism as a development from Kant's "duty". It covers a broad sweep of concepts and shows how they influenced modern man, religion and societies through the ages. https://amzn.to/3gN8zgy $4.19 Kindle 14.95 paperback.

Unkilling Jesus

Who was Paul and what was his role in the creation of Christianity? What was his provenance, and did he meet the resurrected Christ? Who wrote Revelation and what was the document's purpose? Why was Domitian assassinated?

http://amzn.to/2itMCo0 $3.99 Kindle $15.95 softcover

Domitian: The Final Messiah

The central goal of this book is to define the specific themes and concepts that make up Domitian's contribution to Christianity – in a sense, we are defining the specific Domitian overlay to the Christian materials originally developed for Titus.

http://amzn.to/2yWMSlx $2.99 Kindle $6.95 softcover

Paul's Agon and the Mystification of History

Paul and Jesus are joined in one important way; the way of a miracle. They met on the road to Damascus while Paul supposedly pursued Christians. Jesus, in a sense, told Paul to get with the program and stop persecuting his people. In this incident, the Bible tells us that Jesus is already dead, and resurrected. This book argues otherwise.

http://amzn.to/2zSDsuP $5.99 Kindle $19.95 softcover

Christianity on the Arch of Titus

This book explores the "persons" visible on the Triumphant Arch of Titus which is located in the heart of Rome. These people were significant in that they played a role, not only in Rome's conquest of Judaea but also in the creation of Christianity. This book explores those individuals and the roles they played in the creation of one of the most important religious movements in world history.

https://amzn.to/3xz3OgM $3.69 Kindle 10.95 paperback.

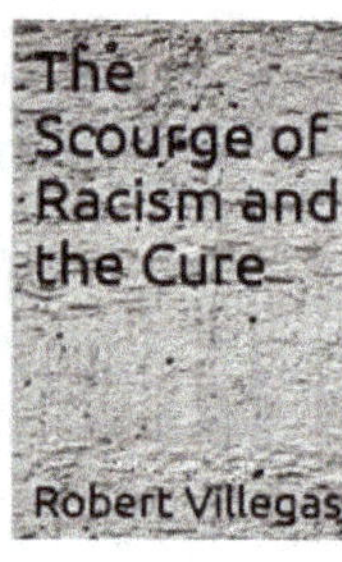

Kant's Atomic Bomb

This book is about Kant's atomic bomb. Obviously, this term is a metaphor utilizing the destructive power of a real atomic bomb to describe the devastation wrought by Kant's philosophy. https://amzn.to/4lvOhX5

Altruism versus Egoism

In this book, I reverse the general view that many people have about both egoism and altruism. Where many people regard altruism as superior morally, I reverse the tables. In my view it is egoism that is morally superior, and I explain here what is good about egoism and what is evil about altruism. https://amzn.to/3TNFiES

The Scourge of Racism – and the Cure

This book could be viewed as a companion work to "What Harvard and Princeton Don't Want You to Know. https://amzn.to/4esVUv7

Effective Altruism – Same Old Altruism

The problem with the new altruism is that it is altruism, nonetheless. This is because the fundamentals of effective altruism are the same as the fundamentals of primordial human sacrifice that began with the decimation of a scapegoat. https://amzn.to/46lYS2q

The REAL Purpose-Driven Life

After centuries of being told that it is not about you, it is time to set the record straight. You are a unique individual and your goal in life should be to achieve your own happiness.
https://amzn.to/2XyrpPf $3.50 Kindle $7.95 softcover

Values and Purpose Workbook

This book is about you. It's about time. After centuries of being told that nothing is about you, it is time to set the record straight. You are a unique individual and your goal in life should be to achieve your happiness. https://amzn.to/2XwlkTv $3.99 Kindle $8.95 softcover

The Real Purpose-Driven Life

After centuries of being told that it is not about you, it is time to set the record straight. You are a unique individual and your goal in life should be to achieve your own happiness. This book is about helping you accomplish your goals and fixing your purpose firmly in place. It covers not only why you should pursue your goals but how to do it.
https://amzn.to/3ebkhjr $3.99 Kindle $6.95 softcover

The Values and Purpose Workbook

Rather than give you tasks that involve doing a lot of things for other people, I'm am going to tell you that focusing on yourself will reveal your life's purpose and express your passions and freedom. I'm going to start with you.
https://amzn.to/3eQf4wG $2.99 Kindle $6.95 softcover

This Book is About You

Some people move briskly bent on a purpose, concerned only about what they are about. Some people walk by them; and do not even notice. They just keep to their path. This book is about you. It's about time. https://amzn.to/3vFMzss
$2.99 Kindle $5.95 softcover

  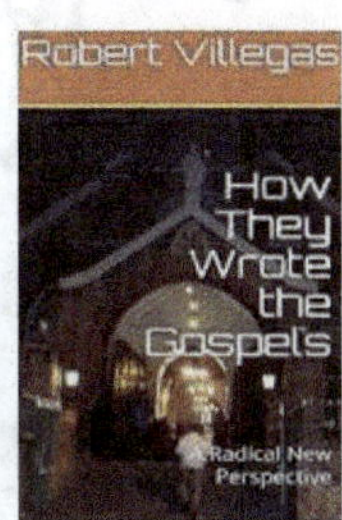 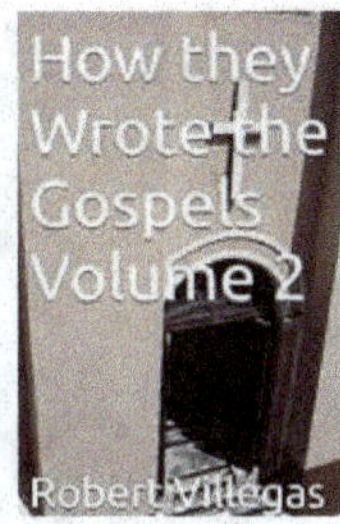

What Paul Did

This book is the shorter version of my book *Paul's Agon*. It seeks to provide a more succinct expression of the key points in that book which is over 500 pages.

The New Jesus Narrative

This book represents one section of my book Unkilling Jesus . I have separated out this section of the book because I believe it can stand alone and make a case that the gospels have been fabricated.

How They Wrote the Gospels Volume 1

This book is Volume 1 of a two-volume work on "How they Wrote the Gospels". It lays the foundation for many of the ideas presented in the companion "Volume 2" book.

How They Wrote the Gospels Volume 2

This second book (How They Wrote the Gospels Volume 2) fulfils the promise of the first volume "How They Wrote the Gospels". This book surveys the literature about how the gospels might have been written.

These three books are based upon a new perspective on the document named Revelation. Based upon a new theory of the story of Jesus as an invention of the Roman Imperial Cult, these books add significant new evidence for this theory.

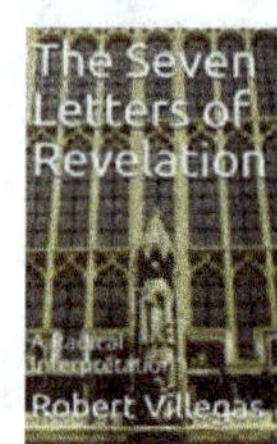

Coded Messages in the Pastorals

The first book in the series on Revelation. I see Christianity, as we know it today, as an outgrowth of mostly one mind and one perspective and that is the mind and perspective of Paul the apostle who was the alter-ego for another man who lived and wrote in the AD 80s and AD 90s. https://amzn.to/3xx2Gdm $4.69 Kindle $10.95 softcover

The Seven Letters of Revelation

The second book on the three-book series on Revelation. The idea that Domitian was the author, through John, of Revelation is a relatively new idea. But, if this is true, it answers many questions about the purpose of Revelation and what events led up to it. By connecting the document to Domitian, we are also able to connect it to Pauline Christianity and understand the context for both Christian writings and Revelation. https://amzn.to/3aLekb4 $3.99 Kindle $6.95 softcover

Understanding the Book of Revelation

The third in the three-book series on Revelation, Understanding the Book of Revelation is the third and final book in the series about the conflict between Paul and Domitian over Paul's version of Christianity which is found in the gospels. https://amzn.to/3tWn6dH $5.19 Kindle $8.95 softcover

Existence a Rational Thoughtbook

A Rational Thoughtbook is designed for thinking as opposed to reading. It combines brief prescient content with stunning imagery. Existence focuses on the nature of existence and gives you intelligent thoughts to integrate into your life.
https://amzn.to/2RZpsKV

The Virtue of Independence

One of the most important goals for any person is to establish intellectual independence. Intellectual independence is the road to "life" independence, which is the ability to earn your own way without help from others. https://amzn.to/3awuCV2

Rational Meditation

Rational Meditation is self-meditation. It is thinking about yourself without guilt and without the tenets of modern philosophy (that the world is unknowable, that man is a phony, that ethics and living are only about others). https://amzn.to/3gus9OE

Understanding the Modern Mind

The purpose of this book is to delve into critical issues about how the human mind has come to the modern position of doubt and despair. The culprits in this matter include the irrationality of both rationalism and skepticism, and, in particular, the child of skepticism known as pragmatism. https://amzn.to/4fd4yyi

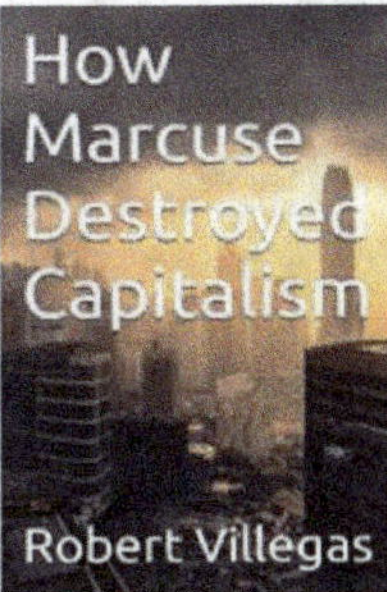

2085 – A City on a River

We live in a city on a river. Our city is called New America, and our river is the river Styx. We have been at war all our lives and all the news is about the war and how our Supreme Leader is winning it.

https://amzn.to/4Oaqi7P

Defending Capitalism

The goal of this booklet is to introduce young people to the economic system known as capitalism. It is my contention that capitalism is the best economic system in the world. The benefits of capitalism have been left out of the discussion in our universities, and I consider this a travesty.

https://amzn.to/4eGBsH6

How Marcuse Destroyed Capitalism

Any human being, in any sphere of activity, who wants to establish a farce, a lie, or an impossible goal, must do so by means of negation. This negation amounts to the evasion of the nature of existence and the misidentification of the facts of reality. https://amzn.to/4eEQNbc

Individualism

Today, our culture is inundated with collectivism, the idea that man belongs to the group. We are told we belong to the family, the community, the church, and the race, etc. We are told that only the collective is important and that sacrifice is the only moral act. This book seeks a different perspective. https://amzn.to/44KAHZf

Poetic Prose and Poetry

These expressions represent some of Mr. Villegas' deepest thoughts as he lived and traveled throughout the world in locations such as Germany (East and West), Austria, Britain, Spain, Canada, France, Luxembourg, Belgium, the Netherlands, Korea, New York, Miami, San Francisco and other locations. https://amzn.to/3vu7X3B $2.99 Kindle $6.95 softcover

The Lost Poems

These poems were discovered among Mr. Villegas's archives in 2016. Many of them have been read by only Mr. Villegas. Most of these poems were rejected as "not that good". After seeing them again, he has changed his mind. These poems expressive, fresh and spontaneously honest. https://amzn.to/3aPg5nB $3.99 Kindle $6.95 softcover

Adam Reborn – A Short Play

Adam Reborn is a play of symbols. Adam and Eve, as I have portrayed them, are young and heroic people learning to deal with a Paradise and God that are hostile to them. There is no chance of life for them. https://amzn.to/3u9Nr8b $2.99 Kindle $6.95 softcover

The Boy Who Stood Alone

Jonny Payne has just discovered Ayn Rand and his parents don't know what to do. They take him to a priest and a psychologist but his only question is "What is the price of independence? https://amzn.to/3nCG6ve $3.99 Kindle $6.95 paperback.

Aphrodite

Johnny is a Spanish guitar player with a mysterious past. At a party, he meets the beautiful songstress Aphrodite who is enthralled with his flamenco guitar skills. Later, she learns they have a connection, a particular song they both appear to know. Aphrodite discovers the connection, and through dreams, the two fall in love. The question is whether they will ever be together. https://amzn.to/3xIlmXZ $3.99 Kindle $5.95 softcover

The Odyssey of Amerigo the Founder

Amerigo was born in a time of desperation and dystopia. He was the only man with the vision of a great future. Many repaired to his cause while others swore to destroy him. They wanted his life, his mind and everything he loved. He swore that no matter what they did, he would win the struggle for freedom and a new future.
https://amzn.to/2Qz8h2t $3.99 Kindle $8.95 softcover

Bob and Bobbie

1967 - a town outside Camp Casey, Korea - two young people have come together to challenge a world that makes love impossible.
https://amzn.to/3sZWSpf $2.99 Kindle $5.95 softcover

The Raven Haired Girl

Bobby met Angie 52 years ago in a poor neighborhood in Indianapolis. It was love at first sight. For a few short months, their relationship blossomed into love. They were in love but didn't know how to be in love because they were only fourteen years old.
https://amzn.to/3306plF $2.99 Kindle $6.95 paperback.

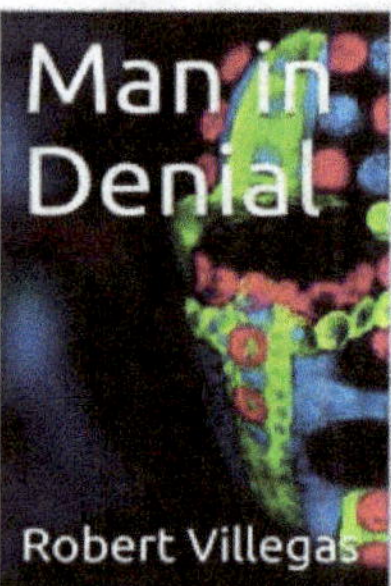

EGOnomics

I believe you need to defend your ego against countless efforts to diminish it. Anti-ego ideologies often equivocate between egoism and narcissism and treat both concepts as if they were the same.

https://amzn.to/45jSzKX

Josephus AKA Peter

The purpose of this book is to establish the theory that the apostle Peter is an alias for the Jewish historian Josephus. To support this view, we must connect both names to the Flavians, and in particular, the Roman general Titus.

https://amzn.to/4kSRb7q

Man in Denial

If psychology has no solid epistemology and metaphysics, how can it stand on its own? I do not think it can and this explains why psychology is in such a sad state today. Yet, before we can put psychology on a solid foundation, philosophy too must advance above the level of puberty. With its base in modern philosophy, even philosophy cannot stand on its own which exposes the real problems with modern psychology.

https://amzn.to/3TUO8kg

Ayn Rand's Moral Code

These pages represent two chapters of my recently updated book, The REAL Purpose-Driven Life plus an additional chapter on good versus evil. https://amzn.to/3lepYi1

Logical Fallacy of Altruism

A logical fallacy is a faulty thought process that violates a rule of proper thinking. A rule of proper thinking is a rule defined by logicians through discovery of logical truths and how to frame good arguments. https://amzn.to/4lvravU

Left versus Right – A False Choice

The enemies of man include both left and right. In order to decide what our futures should be, we must understand what left and right have in common, and what is keeping us from advancing proper principles. https://amzn.to/4ldnZJD

El Boracho

This stage play is about the struggle of the main character, Ricard, who has recently been arrested for driving under the influence (DUI) of alcohol. The play chronicles his personal struggle to deal with how he became an alcoholic and how to repair his life. https://amzn.to/3ZYXkrl

 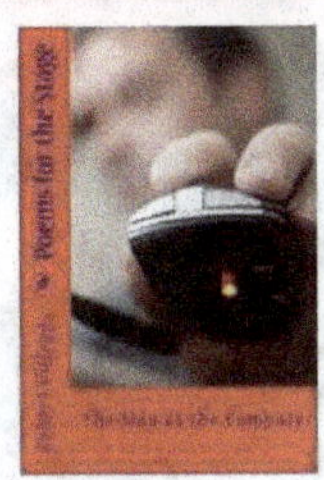

Poems for the Stage – A Story of Love
This dramatic presentation features poems found in Mr. Villegas's book Poetic Prose and Poetry. Some are also found in his book.
https://amzn.to/3gSJctV $2.99 Kindle $5.95 softcover

Poems for the Stage – The Man at the Computer
This dramatic presentation is based upon poems from Mr. Villegas's book Poetic Prose and Poetry. Some of the poems have been slightly altered to reflect the internal story. Mr. Villegas's book Poetic Prose and Poetry can be found on Amazon.com.
https://amzn.to/2R8zpFf $2.99 Kindle $5.95 softcover

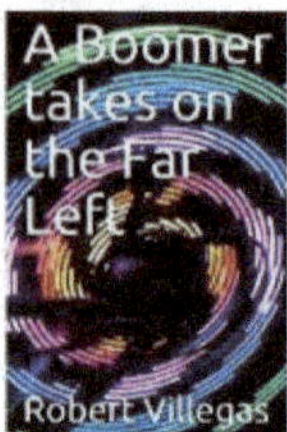   

A Boomer takes on the Far Left

I just learned something about myself – and it isn't very good. In fact, it is very bad. I learned that the opinions of Boomers don't matter any more. We are obsolete in this new age of new knowledge. Anything we think is unimportant and false. I don't think so. https://amzn.to/3tzNqtc $5.19 Kindle $10.95 softcover

Crushing the Alinsky Radicals

The worst enemy of individual rights today is a group of people I call the Alinsky Radicals. These people are now in charge of our culture and temporarily, in charge of government. They are associated, philosophically and politically, with the communists and fascists of the past. They are not your father's liberals. They are the direct descendants of dictators such as Stalin and Mao. In this book, I hope to convince you of the evil of the Alinsky Radicals and to provide the intellectual ammunition you need to eradicate them from society. https://amzn.to/3hbh9WN $3.49 Kindle $8.95 softcover

The Conservative's Dilemma

I wrote this book to ask some important questions about the conservative philosophy of altruism. https://amzn.to/3bfDQ8e $2.99 Kinde $6.95 softcover.

The Biggest Mistakes in History – 2008 to 2016

To be the Chief Executive of the greatest country in the world requires a leader with a great deal of knowledge, experience and reasoning ability. It requires having the very best minds as advisors, minds that the President can count on to give reasoned arguments and detailed knowledge about the important issues of the day. I think it takes a special ability to understand the principle of cause and effect concerning how government action impacts the lives of real people. https://amzn.to/3tDQ4Ol $2.99 Kindle $10.95 softcover

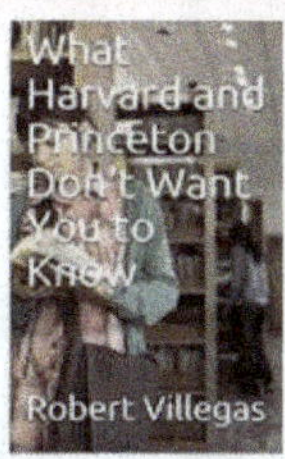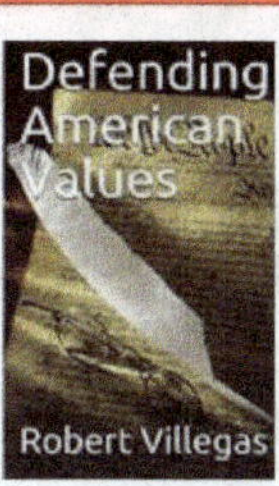

Dachau and Berlin in 1990

This booklet chronicles Mr. Villegas' thoughts during visits to Dachau and Berlin during 1990, disclosing my observations of milestones in German history, past and present, and relating those events to world happenings as they were unfolding at the time. I traveled throughout Germany for much of 1990 while on business. https://amzn.to/3ex578d $2.99 Kindle $6.95 softcover

What Harvard and Princeton Don't Want You to Know

The professors at Harvard and Princeton don't want you to know about the worst ideas in history. This is because they have been pawning these ideas off as true and profound. They have been using them to deceive and manipulate us for centuries. https://amzn.to/3farP5p $5.19 Kindle $9.95 softcover

Defending American Values

This book is made up of several chapters about American values and how they can be defended without a descent into the abyss of dictatorship. The book argues for individual rights and provides reasons why we should fight for them. https://amzn.to/3uMFq9L $3.99 Kinde $5.95 softcover.

Capitalism Doesn't Fail

How many times have we heard the old saw: "Capitalism has failed again" over the course of contemporary events? We heard it during the Great Depression of 1929 after Hoover had invoked tariffs and precipitated economic retaliation and a banking crisis. Along with this question usually came a statement to the effect, that "We can fix capitalism and make it even stronger by issuing economic controls or spending money to stimulate economic activity." https://amzn.to/3xZIAJ6 $4.19 Kindle $10.95 softcover

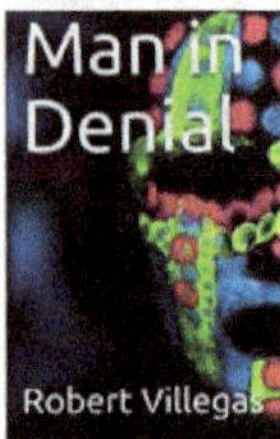

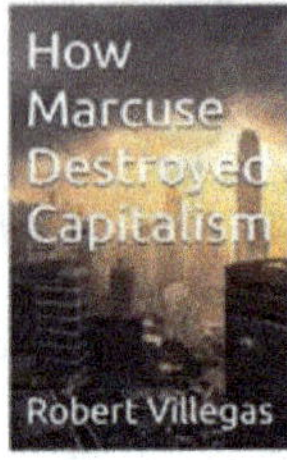

Naming Names in the NT

If psychology has no solid epistemology and metaphysics, how can it stand on its own? I do not think it can and this explains why psychology is in such a sad state today. Yet, before we can put psychology on a solid foundation, philosophy too must advance above the level of puberty. With its base in modern philosophy, even philosophy cannot stand on its own which exposes the real problems with modern psychology. https://amzn.to/3oVTDAQ **$5.99 Kindle $9.95 softcover $18.95 hardcover**

Finding Your Soft Cry

The purpose of this book is to delve into critical issues about how the human mind has come to the modern position of doubt and despair. The culprits in this matter include the irrationality of both rationalism and skepticism, and, in particular, the child of skepticism known as pragmatism.
https://amzn.to/3mRLZF9 **$6.99 Kindle $9.60 softcover $26.95 hardcover**

The New Totalitarianism — Quo Vadis?

One of the fathers of critical theory was Herbert Marcuse who escaped European dictatorship only by coming to America. America gave him the freedom and protection he needed to destroy capitalism in America.
https://amzn.to/2YW9LaS **$4.99 Kinde $8.95 softcover**.

A Call to Reason

A logical fallacy is a faulty thought process that violates a rule of proper thinking. Correct arguments are defined as proper generalized expressions that define logical truths or knowledge. In effect, a rule of logical reasoning addresses all of the common modes of valid argument while the faulty argument contradicts them. This book examines altruism as a logical fallacy.
https://amzn.to/3vdFiB0 **$5.99 Kindle $9.95 softcover $18.95 Hardcover**

Finding Sponsors 1 and 2

This book is written for anyone seeking sponsorship relationships in the sport and entertainment fields. The ideas and principles presented here are applicable to any company, sport team, entertainment company, marketing agency and charitable organization that uses corporate sponsorships to support its activities. Volume 1: https://amzn.to/3ejm1Hp $5.19 Kindle $12.95 softcover Volume 2: https://amzn.to/3eVDo0e $4.69 Kindle $10.95 softcover

How to Write a Sponsorship Proposal

This booklet provide you with some basic guidelines on what to communicate in order to produce a winning sponsorship proposal. These guidelines will focus on what you should be presenting to your potential sponsor to make the best business case for involvement with your team or entertainment company. https://amzn.to/3tpHRxs $2.99 Kindle $6.95 softcover

Hospitality Event Planning Handbook

One key part of your sponsorship activation strategy might be customer hospitality events in conjunction with sporting events. How do you pull off a Hospitality Event for your biggest customers? You may not know how to start, what to do and how to ensure the event is a success. This book can help. http://amzn.to/2mxzpgy $7.95 softcover.

Selling Sponsorship in the Age of the Coronavirus

This book provides suggestions on how sport teams, athletes and concert promoters can mitigate the damage done to their businesses by the economic lockdowns (due to the Coronavirus). It integrates checklists, SWOT Analysis and other valuable business aids into one toolkit that will help you keep your sport and/or genre alive in these difficult times. https://amzn.to/2QVBNiM $5.15 Kindle $5.95 softcover

Finding Sponsors Forms Book

This "Forms Book" is intended to provide samples of the forms mentioned in my book "Finding Sponsors for Sport and Entertainment". This will make it possible for you to reproduce these forms in other formats as well as download the forms document from the SponsorProAZ website for use with Microsoft Word. https://amzn.to/3b95yDW $2.99 Kindle $5.50 softcover

Submitting Your Sponsorship Proposal Online

This booklet enables sport teams and concert promoters to submit their sponsorship proposals to companies that accept only online submission of proposals. https://amzn.to/3euzdti $2.99 Kindle $5.95 softcover

The Art of Sponsorship

This short book is based upon Mr. Villegas' book "Finding Sponsors for Sport and Entertainment". It is also based upon a course that he taught for an organization managing Indiana Parks and Recreation facilities. It is, in a sense, a condensation of information from the book geared toward organizations that would like to earn revenues on their facilities through corporate sponsorship. https://amzn.to/3beuVnC $2.99 Kinde $6.95 softcover.

Restarting Your Business After the Pandemic

This new book is designed to help you restart your business after the Coronavirus pandemic. You will find here all the right questions, how you can find the answers and the forms you need to walk through your restart and coming success. https://amzn.to/2QVBNiM $5.15 Kindle $5.95 softcover